How to Declutter Your Home or Work Office to Improve Productivity

SARAH ADAMS

ISBN-10: 1542859743
ISBN-13: 978-1542859745

CONTENTS

1 INTRODUCTION

For anyone who's ever misplaced an important file, paid a bill late, or simply lost their mind because of a disorganized and cluttered office, this book is for you. Whether disorganization has cost you an important client or caused unnecessary headaches with your boss, we can personally. relate. Decluttering your work space or home office can be quite a grueling endeavor. If organization may not be your calling, these easy to implement, simple ideas and tips, can turn anyone into a decluttering genius. This short book will be your guide to improve productivity and efficiency in the work place. We'll discuss why having an organized office is important, give tips on how to organize and decluttered your space, and provide insight on how to maintain your office for continued productivity. Wouldn't it be wonderful to make the most of your time and become more productive at work? This book will most certainly help you become more efficient and organized at work. Whether you have a home office with finance records, tax returns, and clutter everywhere, a tightly packed, disorderly cubical, or a messy, disheveled work office, let this book help. By organizing and decluttering your work space, not only will you increase productivity, but make the most of your time. No more fumbling through filing cabinets and drawers to find the items you need. This book provides easy to follow, simple ideas to get your home or work office in tip top shape.

2 WHY ORGANIZATION MATTERS

It seems rather obvious why organization matters, yet, so many of us struggle with office organization and clutter. It's important to know why and how being organized can improve productivity before we get started. Have you ever struggled to get tasks and work done in a cluttered, unorganized space? Then you understand the need to re-center yourself and your work space. First, our brains can't function in disorder. When we're organized, we're better able to think and process difficult assignments or problems that arise. With clutter all around, our minds are easily distracted and simple tasks take longer to complete. This cuts down on productivity. Studies show that being able to find everyday items, documents, and more helps improve stress levels. In a disorderly office, the brain is on hyper drive. By getting rid of clutter and improving organization, our bodies can complete tasks rationally and much more quickly and accurately. Think of how many times you've missed a deadline, forgotten an important date, or simply took longer than necessary to find an item or document because of a disarrayed office. Organization matters for office productivity. Being distracted, not able to find what you need, and feeling increased pressure are signs of lack of organization. Now we'll dive into how to start decluttering your work space to improve productivity.

3 GETTING STARTED: STEP BY STEP GUIDE

Now that you know the importance of having an organized office, we can begin the process. Not being able to find the items or documents you need leads to wasted time and energy. In our stress filled lives, why add more fuel to an already burning fire? Decluttering and organizing is good for mental health and vitality. Studies show that being able to find everyday items not only saves time and efforts, but disorganization hinders having a balanced life. If you're overwhelmed by the process of organizing and decluttering, follow these simple steps below for some relief. Read through each before throwing or sorting anything, as the overall goal is to have a clear vision and objective in mind before simply rummaging through your desk and drawers. The first step to an orderly office is to define your work space.

Step 1: Defining the Function and Purpose for Your Work Space

It may seem like a silly question, but ask yourself why you have a home or work office. It seems rather obvious, it's where you do your work, but what kind of work do you do? Think about the purpose of your office and define its function. Is it to do finances, write personal notes, create websites, write stories, meet with clients, design, or something else? Decide what is the function of your office space. If you complete a multitude of tasks each day, divide your office into designated areas. Maybe you've never thought about it before, but not everything has to be completed at your desk.

For example, a lawyer may complete various tasks throughout their day. They may need to complete research, check references, meet with clients, read depositions, and more. Therefore, a lawyer may want to think about having an area in their office where all reference materials are kept, and perform similar tasks in that assigned area. When reading depositions, a small chair in the corner, overlooking a window can serve as a reading or viewing section. If you meet with clients in your office, designate its own space with chairs and whatever else you need.

Designating project areas in your office doesn't mean you need to have a huge space for all the different tasks you complete on a daily or weekly basis. Each profession is different and what an interior designer's assigned areas might be will differ for a photographer. The key is to decide what and where you will complete everyday tasks. Not only will you become more efficient by dividing your office into work stations, but your day will flow better as you move around for some much-needed change in routine. Defining the purpose of your office is the beginning step to getting organized.

Step 2: Making a Game Plan

Now that you have a general idea of the function of your office, it's time to get your hands dirty. In order to create a work space you'll not only use, but love, you need to see the end result and work backwards to achieve a functioning, more productive office. With your vision and purpose clear, it's time to make it a reality. Designate a specific day to work on your office. Schedule it in if you have to. If you make it a priority, it will happen. If, you just dream about a beautiful functioning office and don't do anything about it, it will stay on the backburner. Now's the time to start living a more balanced life, and it can start by getting your home office or work space in order.

The next phase to increase office efficiency begins with taking inventory of what you currently own. This is a great time to get rid of excess items and waste which have been taking up permanent residence in the crevices of your work space or home office far too long.

Step 3: Taking Inventory

After you've considered the function of your home or work office, you'll next need to take stock of all the items and supplies you currently possess. Go through your items and start listing everything you use. You should make a written list of your inventory. This includes paperclips, storage files, pens, reference materials, and more. Now, think about how often you actually use these items. Do you have a drawer full of post-it notes, but you never use them? Do you have a horde of pens and pencils, but you really only write with one or two favorites? Taking inventory helps you realize what you need and what you don't. This will help you minimize supplies for a clutter free desk and work environment. What is the use of having an office full of items or supplies that just sit there, taking up space and becoming an eyesore? Choose supplies and items which serve a purpose.

Step 4: Minimizing Supplies

Again, taking inventory of what you use will greatly help in your decluttering and efficiency efforts. Simply hoarding paper or crafting supplies that haven't been touched in years, is hanging onto to excess items that could go to another home. Your home or work office should act as finely oiled machined, designed to get work done proficiently, professionally, and reduce stress. Another note, don't simply implement items that look pretty, but serve no real purpose. A lovely hole puncher may look great in your office, but if it never gets used, what's the point? It's only taking up space. You can donate all the supplies you don't readily use to someone else. They'll appreciate the gesture, and you can start re-centering yourself and your office space. Yes, your office should reflect your personality and be a space you enjoy being in, but don't go overboard. Having every square inch decorated and bedazzled may be too much. If you haven't minimalized any supplies, but want to add in more decorative items, you might want to reconsider your course. A good rule of thumb, you can't add more items to your office until you let others go.

Step 5: Starting with a Clean Slate

Now that you've minimized supplies, it's time to use some muscle. Begin by clearing out all your supplies and items. This includes clearing out filing cabinets, if possible, chairs, desk, computer, pictures, and whatever else to enable you to start with a clean slate. This will be time consuming and overwhelming at first. Schedule a day or afternoon where you know you'll have sufficient time to declutter and work on your office space. You might need to enlist a friend or colleague for moving heavier items. It would be a good idea to also know where you're going to store all your items in this initial phase. If you can, organize like items and supplies together. This will shorten the amount of time you spend going through everything.

Now it's time to clean, dust, and vacuum. Wipe down blinds, window treatments, and anything else which usually gets neglected. This includes your walls. If your office possesses boring, white walls, give them a thorough wipe down, and they'll shine like new. Dusting cords, electrical plugs, and outlets, and cleaning baseboards is also a good idea. When was the last time your office had a thorough cleaning? Removing dust from your office will help reduce allergens and improve the quality of air you breathe in each day. You spend a considerable amount of time in your office, and whether you're in your home basement or a work cubicle, our bodies can function much better when the air is as clean and fresh as possible.

Step 6: Divide and Conquer

This means to organize all your items and supplies into sections once your office is completely empty. Put all office furniture into one large pile. Again, this will also help you take inventory of what you actually use. If you have a big, bulky filling cabinet, but it's mostly empty, consider using a smaller cabinet or system, so you can get rid of larger furniture taking up space in your office. If you've purchased additional furniture for your office, pile them together with your old items. Allocate another area for all office accessories. This may include that beautiful rug you purchased, lamps, picture frames, and other decorative items. All office supplies should be combined. Pens, stationary, notepads, and stapler should be lumped together. Here are a few other suggested sections to help divide all your office materials and supplies.

Reference Materials
-work policies
-guidebooks
-instruction manuals
-any writing books or resources

Contacts
-client's name and contact information
-address book(s)
-business cards

Finance
-tax records
-spreadsheets
-receipts
-expense reports

Office Supplies
-pens, pencils,
-notebooks, notepads
-stapler, tape, hole puncher, paper clips

Accessories
-frames
-artwork
-decorative storage
-rug

Wall Art
-clock
-certificates/diplomas
-artwork
-chalkboard/white board/pin board
-calendar

Office Essentials
-desk
-storage cabinets
-computer/fax/printer
-chair
-plants
-trash bin
-shredder

Step 7: Moving Items into Your Work Space

Now that you've moved your items and sorted them into like sections, you can now start moving them back in. Start with furniture first. This is the time to consider how you want your office to look. Reorganize to achieve your dream office, if possible. Maybe you never considered moving the desk a different angle. Now's the time to play around with layout. If you want to enlist the ancient practice of Feng Shui, many swear by its power to re-center for improved productivity in the work place.

Also, think about air flow. If you're always freezing in your office because your desk is next to the air vent, move it. If you're always warm because the sun beats through the window during the day, make your office more comfortable to fit your needs. When your body temperature is relaxed and normal, you're able to enjoy your office more readily but also get more done. Choose the best layout for your space, keeping in mind air flow, ventilation, and whatever makes the most sense for your office space.

With your furniture in place, slowly start moving other items back in, one section at a time. Remember, everything should have a purpose and place. You should have already removed excess supplies to help your office stay clutter free once it's beautifully organized. You've taken the effort and time to start fresh, so keep it that way by not putting anything back you know doesn't serve a purpose. This is one of the most time-consuming steps of the process. Moving items back in shouldn't be rushed. Be thoughtful where you place each piece of furniture or item. Is the trash bin easily accessible? Are you putting items you rarely use closest to you or furthest from you? Reference materials are generally kept further from your main hub. Remember, when we discussed dividing your office into different work stations? Does this still apply now that your items are moved back in? Do you still have a section for drafting and designing if you need? Evaluate if you're office is going to fulfill its purpose(s).

Step 8: The Power of Personalization

Decorating is perhaps the most rewarding step of creating a newly improved and functioning office space. Maybe you needed to paint while all your office is in its empty state. We'll discuss the need for glamming up your office later, but nevertheless, it serves as an important step, as it personalizes your space. Once all your everyday items are moved back in, it's time to bring on the accessories. These could be items you specifically purchased to jumpstart your desire to improve your office, or things you previously owned. This adds the finishing touches to your office. They can be artwork you downloaded, accent pieces, a new rug, and more. They make the space more welcoming and personal.

Step 9: Before and After

A picture is worth a thousand words, right? Take a before and after shot of your office space. The transformation will help inspire you to keep your office looking stellar. Over time, you may start gathering clutter again. Pull out the picture of your office looking like a million bucks, and hopefully that will motivate you to do better. These are just a few suggestions to get your office decluttered and organized. You must start with a vison and proceed from there. You may find items and supplies you thought were long lost when you remove everything. Hopefully, these steps will help you take stock in the function of your office space and get your desire for a more proficient office, underway.

4 TIPS FOR KEEPING YOUR OFFICE CLUTTER FREE

Now that we've discussed a few ideas on how to maintain your organized office space, we can dive into tips on how to keep your space clutter free for continued productivity. You don't want your beautiful office becoming an eye sore again? Your office is perfectly organized and strategically thought out. Now, let's keep it that way and learn strategies for storing files, paper, and more.

Storing Paper

Use three basic divisions for storing paper. For example, one pile can be for "finances," one for "turn-in," and another "working on." There should be routine degrees of work involved for any profession. Have a main file for clients, another for projects or assignments, and so on. If your desk and occupation involves extensive paper work, use a filing system which best suits you and your needs to reduce clutter. Paper is the main culprit in creating clutter, therefore, create a paper sorting system which will serve you best. Have file trays on your desk or somewhere in your office. Not only will you be able to locate a file, but it will train your brain to organize paperwork per your sorting system.

Organizing Files

Only keep files you need. If you haven't used a file in a year or so, get rid of it. This applies to desktop files on your computer or laptop as well. If you have hard copies of files, truly evaluate if you need to keep storing them. Think about combining files with other colleagues. If they can store something you may need in a future time in their office, go for it. Borrowing what you may need down the road, instead of keeping an item, will also reduce office clutter. Many people hoard tax returns from 10 years. Truthfully, you only need to keep two years back of tax returns and other similar information. Holding onto excess clutter only holds you back and can pull you down like a gravitation force.

Organizing Digital Files

Organize computer and digital files daily. Anytime you save or create a new document, make sure you clean up your desktop. Having photos, documents, and more swarming your computer screen initiates chaos. It welcomes it in like a moth to a flame. Not only does it waste the time you could be spending doing other tasks, searching for files and not knowing where you saved them is frustrating. It's also suggested to understand your computer to the best of your ability. What is backup storage? Should I use a thumb drive? What if I save my documents under a different option? These are all great questions, and it could benefit you greatly to answer them.

Understanding the technology inside and out you use every day will also help you become amazingly productive at work. Efficiency comes when your office is streamlined like a finely oiled machine. The gears all work in harmony to push through with as much ease as possible. You want your office to function likewise. Therefore, create folders on your desktop, organize them weekly or better yet daily before leaving your work space. The time and headache it will save, will literally only take a few minutes each day.

Scanning Hard Copies

Another tip to reduce paper clutter is to save hard copies electronically to a desktop or thumb drive. While it may be time consuming to scan and then save documents, the joy in getting rid of clutter is well worth it. Again, clean up your computer files regularly and you'll always be able to find anything, anytime. With computer files, if you haven't used a document in a year, and don't anticipate using it any longer, delete it. Clear up your storage space and keep your computer or laptop functioning much more proficiently. Saving hard copies electronically doesn't take much effort, and will greatly reduce paper clutter easily.

Storage and Filing Solutions

Use files and office storage sensibly. Maybe you wanted open shelving in your office to display beautiful boxes, but they remain empty. Utilize every square inch of your office. Put paper in those storage boxes, or important items you use often, but don't want scattered all over your desk. If you have storage, use it. This will not only keep your desk clutter free, but help you become more organized. Also, store hard copies in organized files which make the most sense. Don't store fiancé records in a client's file, as they don't go together. If you can, keep files on a thumb drive or computer. You will greatly reduce the amount of clutter that can accumulate in your office. When you cleared out and organized your office initially, these sorts of things should have been handled, but remember to keep and store all items and files sensibly.

Eliminating Clutter

Don't have a junk drawer to catch all things. Many of us have a junk drawer lurking where every day items just seem to end up. Like a gravitational pull, the junk drawer may be the most random drawer in the home or office. To be as proficient as possible, eliminate the need of a junk drawer in your work space. This is the reason you utilized storage options and organized all your materials in the first place, Remember, time is a precious thing, and you don't need to waste it shuffling through various items, searching for one thing. This leads to the next tip.

Another way to eliminate clutter is to shred papers or documents you no longer need. Some may keep papers piled up for weeks or months before getting them to the shredder. Do so immediately to remove any sign of clutter from your home or work office. This also goes for junk mail. Maybe you meant to save a newspaper clipping with a coupon in it. If you haven't used it within a week or two, simply shred it or recycle it. Eliminate clutter before it starts piling up. If you do find something worth keeping or you intend to use, keep it stored in your filing system, perhaps under "working on." Another tip is to pin it to your wall organization, so you'll see it and remember to use it. Be sure to declutter your pin board however, weekly so it's purpose promotes efficiency and not just a cluttered mess on the wall.

Defining Purpose

Each drawer has a purpose and home. When you envisioned your dream office, did it have a random drawer to catch a variety of items? Was it cluttered, filled with office supplies, mints, and crackers? Hopefully your answer is no. You envisioned an office where everything had a purpose and a home. If you don't know where to put an item, create a home for it. In your desk drawers, you should have notepads, paper, writing utensils, and any other items you use regularly. Your pens or pencils might be stored in a decorative holder, or you have organization sections in your drawer for supplies. If you don't, make it a point to purchase drawer dividers, so your items have a definite home. Your co-workers will gasp at how organized your office space is, and clients will appreciate your ease at helping them when it comes to being decluttered and organized at work.

Office Common Sense

The items closest to you are the items you use readily. It wouldn't make sense to store your reference materials inside your desk, when you use them maybe once or twice a month, would it? It also wouldn't make sense to keep your writing supplies in a filing cabinet the furthest from you. Therefore, be smart about where you place your items. We've discussed this, but think about your office in regards to different work stations. Items used in those stations should remain and be utilized in those stations. It's important to make your office work for you. If what you envisioned isn't really working, adjust for a much more structured and streamlined office.

Keeping Cords Orderly

Keep cords untangled. You've seen offices where cords are a jumbled eyesore of wires and mayhem. Maybe that once or still is your office now. Creating a visually appealing space where cords are untangled and hidden is like a visual magic trick. Hiding cords instantly makes your office appear much more uncluttered and organized. Enlisting devices which will keep your cords untangled and hidden will help your office appear much more organized. It's a great way to spruce up your office quickly and without much effort. There are several other tips for staying organized and maintaining your office space. For now, these tips should suffice and give you the encouragement needed to make your office one amazing space.

5 PRODUCTIVITY TIPS

With your office organized and cleaned, you'll be sure to find the items you need to become much more proficient at work. When you feel secure and comfortable in your office, you should be able to get tasks completed more quickly and efficiently. Decluttering your work space doesn't have to be the only tip to improve efficiency. Here are further suggestions on how to be productive in your work space for double the effect.

Racing the Clock

Schedule your time for each day's tasks. For example, decide how long you need to spend responding to emails, calling clients, doing finances, and whatever else. To be diligent, you can set a timer, and insist on moving onto your next set of items, once your allotted time has run out. This will help you prioritize your time and keep you moving. It breaks up your day so it doesn't become as monotonous. Also, it can motivate you to get tasks completed before the timer runs out, sort of like a little game.

Prioritizing and Time Management

You can also utilize vertical wall organization such whiteboards, chalkboards, and pin boards. They serve as reminders for everyday or major items that need to get completed, but you can also divide your time by using these items. Large calendars are also helpful, as you can see your schedule out months at a time. This will help you not to double book clients, and you can quickly glance to see what you have planned, instead of trying to piece it all together from a plethora of post-it notes. Vertical wall organization is easy to write or erase notes, and you can feel great accomplishment when you get to check something off your list. It not only lets you see what's on your plate, but colleagues and clients can see as well. When you utilize the assistance of wall organization, you can see your day clearly. This helps boost productivity as you visually are reminded of important tasks.

Prioritize what needs to get accomplished first. When you make a list of all your work priorities, you can see items most crucial to get accomplished and can schedule your time accordingly. There's only so much you can complete in your day, so if you know a certain assignment will take two hours to finish, plan accordingly. Prioritizing is perhaps one of the hardest things for many, but if you don't prioritize, you don't know if you have the proper time to get tasks completed, or if you can take on new projects or clients. Prioritizing also helps to realize what's most important. You can see your life on paper and perhaps drop things that take up too much of your time. When you realize just how much you have overcommitted yourself, it can serve as a great reminder to break free from things tying you down. Take in all your priorities and balance those accordingly so you still have a life outside of work.

Delegating

Delegate tasks if possible. This may not be possible for some, but if you're able to delegate tasks to an assistant or fellow colleague do what you must to save time and energy. Sharing responsibilities can go a long way in a person's everyday work environment. Maybe it's your turn to take a client out for dinner, but you have other commitments. Ask a partner to switch with you and you'll do it next time. This can save headache and stress in the office, if you're able to delegate tasks. Maybe you need to show a client a house. If a fellow real estate agent is close by, they can let your clients in, and you can meet them shortly after. Think of ways in which you can save time, without compromising your job duties to become as efficient as possible.

Utilizing Technology to Increase Proficiency

Utilize headsets, software programs (speech to text), and more to get work done faster. There are many software programs which can make your work life easier. One of them being a headset, so you can type while you talk to clients. You can get a briefing done, while doing research, as your hands are free to do other tasks. For many people, they've found speech to text software programs to be lifesavers. Simply talk and your text is written for you. That's it. There may be a few quirks involved when initially trying out and setting up software, but once you're all finished, think of how much easier your day can flow with technology. You may not be the fastest typist, therefore, utilizing different software programs is a great solution to get more work done faster. There are other programs which format spreadsheets, greatly cutting down time with finances. Another great time saving tip is to utilize pre-made emails, contact forms, and more that you seem to type repeatedly. Make templates for your everyday tasks to complete your work much more quickly.

Keeping Track of Office Supplies

Take weekly inventory of ink levels and other office supplies. Reorder anything you need. How many times have you gone to print something, only to realize your ink levels are low? Many often don't think about the little things that keep offices running smoothly, but are essential to being productive. Don't be caught unprepared anymore. It not only can display your lack of preparation and attention to detail, but you may miss deadlines due to not taking proper inventory of your office supplies. To always keep moving forward with assignments and tasks, take inventory of what you have, and reorder what you need. Take written note of your office inventory. It will save time and heartache if you're always prepared. If you had to make fifty brochures for a convention, could your printer handle it? Think of "what if" scenarios and evaluate if your office could perform such tasks. Taking weekly inventory of your office supplies is one of the best ways to becoming more efficient.

Thank-You Notes

Have thank you notes handy for a personalized touch to clients and colleagues. This adds a sense of gratitude and humanness to you. Thank you notes are rarely utilized today as much as they were in the past. With text messages, emails, and other digital devices, how much more does it mean to someone to receive a hand written thank you note? It shows you're able to step outside the technological world and realize people are still people and require a personal touch or connection every now and again. By having thank you notes handy, you can easily make connections with clients or colleagues and grow in your networking relationships. Many companies make fun, personal stationary which can match your personality. You can spark up someone's day by sending a hand-written thank you note. Storing them somewhere in your office you'll see daily, will remind you to look for reasons to send them to clients, colleagues and friends.

Notetaking

Become a master notetaker. Keep a notepad with you always, just in case. You never know when an idea may strike, or when you need to remember something for work. Having your personal notebook is like your extra brain. When your real brain can't remember something, you hopefully have your notebook to refer to. When you meet with clients, go to a staff meeting, or ideas come to you whenever you're not in the office, you'll be glad you had something to write your thoughts down. It also shows a level or your commitment around the office and will garnish a reputation for being meticulous and prepared for anything. Your smartphone can serve as your constant go-to companion, yet good old fashioned notebook and pen seems to always do the trick.

6 HOW TO MAINTAIN YOUR ORGANIZED WORKSPACE FOR CONTINUED PRODUCTIVITY

After you've followed the steps to a clutter free and organized office, don't stop there. Maintaining your work space may be harder than decluttering it. Many people keep their work space organized for a time, but fall back into former habits. Don't let this become you. Your office looks stellar, amazing even. Here are a few tips to help you maintain your work space for continued productivity.

Eating at your desk?

If you eat at your desk, keep a mat close by. Eating at your desk may be your only chance at nourishment throughout your busy day. Simply make use of a table mat to keep your desk crumb free. When you're finished, clean it quickly and place the mat back into your storage. It helps establish a routine mentally by making the mat separate from your work space. Temporarily it serves to make you feel as if you're not at your desk totally. When you're done, it signals to your brain to go back into work mode. Blurring eating and working can make the day drag longer and not provide you with what your lunch break is intended for. It's also a good idea, to not eat where you work, if you can possibly help it. It's the same with not working where you sleep. These are two separate tasks, and again, blurring the two makes the action lose its purpose. Our next tips tie into keeping your desk clean, after eating at your desk, or not.

Daily Checklist

This could include a detailed list of all the things to complete before shutting down the office each day, or perform on a weekly basis. You must work a little every day to ensure your office stays as organized as it is now. You've done so much work to shuffle through unused items, donate others you don't, and clean and spruce up your space, don't let it go to waste weeks or months from now. Clean and declutter every day for best results. Train yourself to throw paper away or shred documents immediately, before they start piling up and you've lost your brain again. You can always make it a priority to declutter at the end of the day before going home.

Routine Cleaning

Set a timer and start cleaning the week's or day's clutter. This is one way to remind yourself to spruce up your office. Schedule the time in your day. The point is, remind yourself to keep items organized. If you notice you haven't put files where they need to go, take the time to do so as soon as possible. It's often easier to declutter and organize when things haven't gotten out of control yet. Remember that picture you first took of your improved, clutter free office? Now's the time to remember how things should always resemble. Try to recreate that picture to the best of your ability. Take pride in how hard you worked to organize and declutter your office. Using a timer is a simple, yet effective way to declutter your office in a matter of minutes. Your co-workers may think you a little zany as you race the clock to declutter your space, but by keeping organized, you will be so much more productive at work and can work in a space that is serene, and streamlined to get work done. When you come to work each day to an organized, clutter free office, you'll reap the rewards a little sprucing up each day offers.

Cleaning Supplies

Another helpful tip is to assign a home or place for your office cleaning supplies. When it comes to decluttering, organizing, and cleaning your office, having the appropriate supplies certainly helps. Keep cleaning wipes, dusting cloths, and whatever else to ensure you keep your equipment and space working as efficiently as possible. Clear away dust from your keyboard regularly, tighten cords, and more. If you designate one desk or drawer for cleaning supplies, you may be more inclined to remember to clean. Remember to take stock of cleaning supplies along with other office inventory so you are always able to keep your space sparkling. It takes time and effort to keep your office clean, and even if you do have some janitorial personnel come in at the end of the day, they probably won't detail your office the way you should. It's your office and your responsibility if you want it to stay in tip top shape. It takes little time to do a quick weekly cleaning, but well worth it.

7 GIVE YOUR OFFICE SPACE PERSONALITY

You've made your office much more organized and functional to increase productivity. Now, these tips below offer ideas to add personality and interest to your office space. We all want an office that dazzles. By adding in a few personal touches, it helps your home or work space not to feel so sterile. It welcomes clients, makes you appear appealing to colleagues and others, and showcases your individuality.

Why Your Office Space Needs Personality

Your office needs personality because it makes going to work more exciting when you feel at home while getting tasks and assignments completed. Our brains can do more work when they're pleased or not easily distracted. If your office lacks color or personality, our brain connects it with the mundaneness of work. We don't get excited and therefore, our pace is slowed down. Being motivated, happy, and inspired has a great deal to do with becoming more proficient at work. It's not just for the visual eye, but for mental health. If you feel like you work in a dungeon, does creativity really flow? If you're stark office doesn't make you happy, try adding a little personality to it. With artwork, a new paint color, and more, you can let your creativity soar. It's your space to accomplish all the things you need to. Make it one you enjoy being in as much as you possibly can. Adding personality can also create an environment which reduces stress. If your goal is to create a more serene, calming space, you'll feel it, even when overwhelming projects or assignments arise. Just how do you add personality? It can start by visualizing and pinning ideas you like for office storage and other images on the web. Here are a few more ways to find inspiration for your office space.

Using Apps for Decorating

Many may want to add personality to their office space, but don't know how to go about it. Think about what you envision your office to look like. Do you dream of relaxing colors and pretty embellishments? Or, are you more practical and long for an efficient, modern space? Picking a style can add to the overall mood of your office, and improve your spirits or add motivation. If you've used the online app Pinterest before, then you're no stranger to the world of inspiration it offers for just about anything. Pinterest is an online platform, and amazingly easy to join and use. Plus, it's free. It's a way to save images on the web and organized them. You'll find loads of beautiful home and work office images. Create a board and start pining to your heart's content. After you've pinned a few pictures, you'll realize your overall look and mood for your office. If you can't paint the walls of your work office, you can still find ideas for supplies, embellishments, quotes, artwork, and more on Pinterest. Even adding a rug, accessories, a lamp, and pictures will create a welcoming, personalized environment. Start gaining an idea of what you imagine your dream office to resemble. Pinterest is one way to help gather ideas.

When you find the ideal image of the office of your dreams, make notes of what you need to replicate it. You can then go shopping for similar office supplies, accessories, and whatever else. When you click on your pins, you be should be taken directly to the original blog or website the image came from. There, you can often find the specific paint color, rug, and whatever else you pinned, and where you can purchase items. Pinterest can make it amazingly easy to find ideas and inspiration to create the office of your dreams.

Besides Pinterest, you can also find office inspiration on the Instagram. You simply download the free app if you don't have it, set up an account, and search for office ideas. Maybe you have friends with perfectly organized spaces. You can check out their photos and photos of others by doing a simple search. Either Pinterest or Instagram are great for finding storage solutions and more.

Buying Office Organization

The key to buying office furniture and organization is to keep it simple. Accessories can go a long way in personalizing a space. A great way to add personality is to find a picture of an office space you'd like to replicate. Have a game plan in mind for the items you'd like to purchase. Decide what purpose it will serve so you don't simply buy something for the sake of buying it. Some like to make a sketch of their office before they purchase accessories and furniture. You should also take measurements to ensure your purchases will fit. It'd be detrimental to know where you're going to hang diplomas or other certifications ahead of time. It also helps to visualize your office first, so you have an end vision in mind. Remember, anything you add to your office should have a purpose. If you can, search for deals and sales. Decluttering and organizing is great, but so is saving money while doing it.

Decorating Your Office on a Budget

If buying fancy stationary, gold accent pieces, decorative supplies, and more isn't within your budget, there are many ideas out there to make your office super chic, stylish, and personalized without breaking your pocket book. Finding items such as empty food canisters, glass jars, yogurt cups, and more can help you become more organized on the cheap. There are many tutorials online on how to spray paint or glam up storage items and accessories. There are also free printables on the web to add personality and motivational quotes to your office space. Here is some free artwork found on Pinterest with a simple search *free office printables*. Many blogs such as "Be Creative" and "Remodelaholic" offer great office decorating tips and free printable artwork when you need to design your office on a budget.

If you're looking for cheap office furniture and supplies, Ikea is a great company for sturdy, yet affordable office items. They offer their services to many different countries and online delivery, in case you're not near one of their stores. Read reviews before you purchase items and be sure to measure your space before buying. There are many "Ikea hacks" out there on how to paint, revamp, and repurpose many Ikea items to customize an office space perfect for you. If you're looking to add personality to your office on the cheap, Ikea can help.

Revisiting Your Vision

Now that you've purchased a few items to spruce up your space to add personality, make sure you still have your original vision and game plan in mind. If you have way too many accessories and your space is only going to be a stylish cluttered mess, re-access. It always helps to have a vision in mind before decluttering a space. Your office can be anything you dream, just ensure it's functional, organized, and streamlined so you can be as productive as possible.

8 CONCLUSION

Hopefully you've gain some insight and ideas to make your work space not only a dream space, but more streamlined to increase productivity. From gathering ideas from the web, to defining the function of your home or work office, to making a weekly or daily checklist, you can not only create a clutter free office space, but maintain it. Hopefully there's no more fumbling through drawers to find a file or unnecessary headaches with clients or bosses. Our hope is to help you create a more relaxed, functional, and professional work space. Whether you're meeting clients, drafting a new story, or working on finances, your office space should be your sanctuary. Remember, it only takes a few minutes every day to eliminate clutter and become much more productive at work. With clutter out of your office, you can live a much more balanced life, being able to time manage and get tasks done efficiently. By following these tips, never misplace an important file, pay a bill late, or lose your mind again. Utilize these ideas to the best of your ability and happy decluttering!

Printed in Great Britain
by Amazon